BY JOHN ASHBERY

Some Trees, 1956
The Tennis Court Oath, 1962
Rivers and Mountains, 1966
Fragment, 1969
A Nest of Ninnies
    (with James Schuyler), 1969
The Double Dream of Spring, 1970
Three Poems, 1972

JOHN ASHBERY

THE VERMONT NOTEBOOK

JOE BRAINARD

Los Angeles
BLACK SPARROW PRESS
1975

for Doug Crase

Acknowledgements: parts of this book were published previously in ZZ magazine, edited by Kenward Elmslie, and in *Statements: New Fiction from the Fiction Collective*, George Braziller, Inc.

LIBRARY OF CONGRESS CATALOGING IN PUBLICATION DATA

Ashbery, John.
    The Vermont notebook.

    "250 hardcover copies numbered & signed by the author & artist."
    I. Brainard, Joe, 1942-   ill. II. Title.
PS3501.S475V4   818'.5'407   75-1042
ISBN 0-87685-227-4
ISBN 0-87685-226-6 pbk.

The Vermont Notebook

October, November, December.

The climate, the cities, the houses, the streets, the stores, the lights, people.

Industrial parks, vacant lots, yards, enclosures, fields, arenas, slopes, siding, tarmac, blacktop, service roads, parking lots, drive-in deposits, libraries, roller rinks, drag racing, karting, plazas, reflecting pools, evergreen hedges, war memorials, turn-arounds, supermarkets.

Bridge clubs, Elks, Kiwanis, Rotary, AAA, PTA, lodges, Sunday school, band rehearsal, study hall, book clubs, annual picnics, banquets, parades, brunches, library teas, slide lectures, seances, concerts, community sings.

Gulf Oil, Union Carbide, Westinghouse, Xerox, Eastman Kodak, ITT, Marriott, Sonesta, Crédit Mobilier, Sperry Rand, Curtis Publishing, Colgate, Motorola, Chrysler, General Motors, Anaconda, Crédit Lyonnais, Chase Manhattan, Continental Can, Time-Life, McGraw Hill, CBS, ABC, NBC.

Paraphernalia, Tapemeasure, Dorothée Bis, La Boutique Alice Schweitzer, Crouch and Fitzgerald, Gump's, Sibley, Lindsay & Curr, Strawbridge & Clothier, Hecht's, Sutter's, the Eighth Street Bookshop, Plummer McCutcheon, Ovington's, Révillon, Hector's, Nathan's, Soup Burg, Blum's, Nedick's, Fraser-Morris, Charles & Co., Fauchon, Colette's.

Grey, ocher, mauve, gentian, tabac, beige, greige, buff, taupe, mastic, fawn, havane, verdigris, smoke, amber, russet, outremer.

Beggar-my-neighbor, pounce, fish, old maid, progressive euchre, bezique, backgammon, mah jongg, dominoes, hearts, contract bridge, Michigan poker, rummy, solitaire, Monopoly, Sorry, Parcheesi, Scrabble, Authors, checkers, Chinese checkers, chess, go, fan tan, honeymoon bridge.

Murder, incest, arson, rape, grand larceny, extortion, forgery, impersonating an officer, resisting arrest, loitering, soliciting, possession of a controlled substance, drunken driving, reckless endangerment, slander, mental cruelty, non-assistance of person in danger, perjury, embezzlement, sodomy, child abuse, cruelty to animals, bootlegging, adultery, bigamy, bearing false witness.

Charlottesville, Washington, Baltimore, Macon, Manassas, Asheville, Wheeling, Roanoke, Richmond, Charleston, Savannah, Atlanta, Chattanooga, Tallahassee, Tampa, Orlando, Daytona, Jacksonville, Miami, Miami Beach, Key West, Key Biscayne, West Palm Beach, Lake Wales.

Dallas, Fort Worth, Houston, San Antonio, Waco, El Paso, Corpus Christi, Galveston, Amarillo, Baton Rouge.

Norman, Enid, Tulsa.

Regina, Medicine Hat, Edmonton, Winnipeg, Calgary.

The New York Times, The New York Daily News, The New York Post, Woman's Wear Daily, The Times of London, The London Sunday Times, The Observer, The Sunday Telegraph.

Maggie and Clyde Newhouse, Egon von Furstenberg, Bill Blass, Rex Reed, Pauline Trigere, Betsy Theodoracopoulos, Nan Kempner, Chessie Rayner, Arthur and Elaine Cohen, Huntington Hartford, Bobo Rockefeller, Lady Malcolm Douglas Hamilton, Jacques Kaplan, Larry Rivers, Howard Kanovitz, Alex Katz, Lawrence Rubin, William Rubin, Robert and Ethel Scull, Paul Cornwall Jones, Brook Alexander, Kynaston McShine, Pierre Apraxine, Ruth Kligman, Jackson Pollock, Lee Krasner Pollock, Willem de Kooning, Elaine de Kooning, Fairfield Porter, Anne Porter, Robert Dash, Jane Freilicher, Jane Wilson, John Gruen, Leonard and Felicia Bernstein, Gold and Fizdale, Eleanor Steber, Patrice Munsel, Irra Petina, Adolph Gottlieb, Norman Bluhm, Michael Goldberg, Patsy Southgate, Peter Matthiessen, Grace Borgenicht, Warren Brandt, Marilyn Fischbach, Aladar Marberger, Mr. and Mrs. Robert Sabel, Aaron Frosch, Lee Eastman, Benjamin Sonnenberg, Harold and May Rosenberg, Stella Adler, David and Ellen Oppenheim, Lukas and Cornelia Foss, Mr. and Mrs. Thomas B. Hess, Jolie Gabor, Col. and Mrs. Serge Obolensky, Bessie de Cuevas, Mr. and Mrs. Seymour Halpern, Morris Golde, Aaron and Irene Diamond, Joseph Mackles, Willard Cummings, Richard and Paula Benjamin, Bricktop.

Anne Waldman, Tom Veitch, Hilton Obenzinger, Jack Marshall, Kathleen Fraser, Sandra MacPherson, Anne Sexton, Maxine Kumin, Robert Lowell, Elizabeth Bishop, A. R. Ammons, Ed Sanders, Kenward Elmslie, Nancy Ellison, Sandra Hochman, Arthur Gregor, Kenneth Koch, James Schuyler, Maureen Owen, Carter Ratcliff, Gerrit Henry, John Ashbery, Jim Dine, Alan Senauke, Louis Zukofsky, Jackson MacLow, Emmett Williams, Dick Higgins, David Antin, Jerome Rothenberg, Joanne Kyger, Robert Creeley, Bill Berkson, Ebbe Borregaard, Tom Clark, Lewis MacAdams, Barbara Guest, Robert Bly, Donald Hall, Donald Justice, David Wagoner, Richard Howard, Joe Brainard, Helen Adam, Charlie Vermont, Paul Violi, Daniela Joseffi, Allen Planz, James Tate, Elinor Wylie, Ron Padgett, Charles Bukowski, Mark Strand, Daisy Aldan, David Shapiro, Albert Herzing, Edward Field, Scott Cohen, Tom Weatherly, Diane di Prima, David Meltzer, Allen Ginsberg, Gregory Corso, Peter Orlovsky, LeRoi Jones, David Henderson, Bernadette Mayer, Vito Acconci, John Perreault, George Montgomery, Jennifer Bartlett, Rochelle Ratner, Rochelle Owens, Diane Wakoski, Marya Zaturenska, Muriel Rukeyser, Douglas Crase, David Kermani, George Oppen, David Ignatow, Fanny Howe, Marge Piercy, Erica Jong, Adrienne Rich, John Hollander, James Wright, Jean Valentine, Margaret Atwood, Margaret Randall, W. S. Merwin, Lawrence Ferlinghetti, Eugene MacCarthy, Louis Untermeyer, Theodore Holmes, Joel Oppenheimer, Gilbert Sorrentino, Aram Saroyan, Scott Burton, Leonard Cohen, Bob Dylan, Rod McKuen, Bruce Gilmour, Carolyn Kizer, Russell Edson, Hugh Seidman, Charles Simic, Bill Zavatsky.

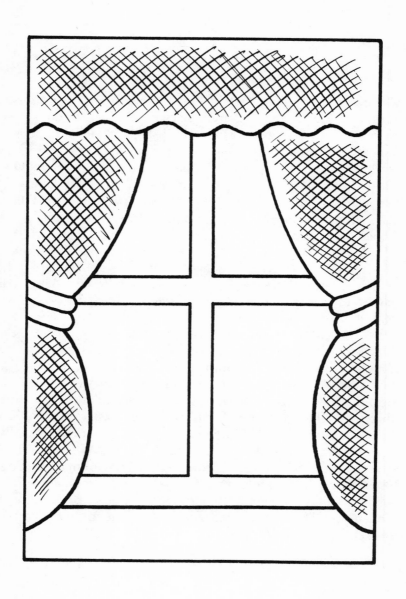

Front porches, back porches, side porches, door jambs, window sills, lintels, cornices, gambrel roofs, dormers, front steps, clapboards, trees, magnolia, scenery, McDonald's, Carrol's, Kinney Shoe Stores.

Suede, tweed, cotton, silk, jersey, whipcord, cavalry twill, melton, moire, nylon, net, challis, cordovan, maxi, midi, scarf, shoes, zipper, cuff, button.

Darkness, eventide, shadows, roost, perch, leaf, light, evasion, sentinel, plug, dream, mope, urchin, distress, ways, many, few, found, dreaming, unclad, season, solstice, many, before, few, undid, seam, artery, motor, before, sleep, come, mouth, asshole, behaving, foundered, sleep, reef, perfect, almost.

Jewelers say that some lie on the heights. They say that some go unnoticed long gone on the heights. Jewelers say we cannot long understand what goes on on the heights. They say we are treason to understand what goes on not to understand what goes on. They say gals understand more. They say guys understand more. They say guys and gals glued to surprise partition understand more. They say all understand more. They say no one understand more. Me and guys prefer going on lazy new heights understanding more. Me and guys go on long road now out of gone understanding your lore. You and gals participate in midsummer frolic in order to understand your. Your behalf. You frolic in midsummer wind on behalf. I in November am a beaver on no one's behalf. Because I am a beaver I see with a beaver's eyes. I think with a beaver's mind. I read books on beavers. I see the light as it manifests itself to beavers. I object on behalf of beavers. I am thrown down long canyon into sight just out of sight of beeches. If there were any to crave beeches they might. But there is no one only the long cascade of horses. I lie now at the cypress roots crying. Crying for my lost love my lost appearances as the weeds wave faithfully volunteering as they can one after the other. The book I read is the dump it is printed in dump letters. As the wind on dump light so the acid red light of wells of dump leaves. I tell the old story of the dump. I work on the story to be the real story of the dump which is never telling. If it ever was telling it would not be the dump which it is. The dump escapes the true scape of the telling and in so doing it is its own scape—the dump dumped and dumping. As I swear the dump is my sweet inner scape self so do I condone the dump for having nothing left for me only the will to go on dumping creating it out of its evacuation. I will go to the dump. I am to be in the dump. I was permanently the dump and now the dump is me, but I will be permanently me when I am no longer the dump air. The dump air lasts.

31

Tobacco lands squaring off hilly landscapes hovered on by piper cubs and always a bit of rainbow beginning. Why not ending? I dunno. You said it. No I didn't. You did too. I did no such thing. Now it is ending. The trees have their galoshes, the little boxes where the newspaper is delivered. It was good to be home at last but this was no home it was the home of tomorrow. Uneaten, inside out in a word. Bang on the air went the sparrow. Little Johnny ran in the house. The man in the hall. The red spider against the pane. How dark the furniture in his brain ticked off against the crisscrosses of apology trying to happen against the strangeness of invented circumstances. This was no way. Tomorrow breathed. There is an island called today you can wish it away it is a blob of tear plopped simply awful on the grass. Wish away.

Sometimes the weary traveler suffering from jetlag prefers to be shown directly to his hotel to be sewn in the sheets from which no dream ever befalls. Weary and heartsick, emotionally battered by the voyage, the eyes overcome with fatigue, unable to read the newspaper thoughtfully provided for him he teeters on the hem of sleep, disrobing this way or that, clenching in his teeth all those distraught objects of the recent past—the way someone looked at him, seeming not seeing but just seeing. The sandwich the way it was. The coffee, how much better or how much worse than the last time. The clerk peeping at his papers. These collect and dissipate like gnats on a screen door—some penetrate the holes in the screen, others move on outside and are replaced by new shoals and whorls, but the movement is the same, grudging giving and giving back. So many marvelous empty mountains. So much eye, such frivolity. The ultimate lightness.

Permeation, ventilation, occlusion.

Red sandstone cliffs reaching higher than the sky.

We are glad that you could come. It is nice that you are here. We are glad to have you with us. And now you must come again. We are sorry that you must go, and happy to have extended our hospitality to you.

Ripe for the eye. Flowering in places. It is empty and big handed. The morning beats time for it. All things are secretly bored. It is seen that the rhythm scans itself the traveler only changes the sky. The high-flying clouds are eyewash.

Another day. Who knew what it was up to in the brush. It has come a long way, wrought and continues to wreak changes that continue to get in the way. They are the land, what it once was. I like looking off to my right, seeing something I had known seeing, and to the left the sky changes, is changing, as a twig in spring. Dark sails over me. I know no one. No place is planted, gets up and starts on again. Nowhere beside the puddle. I get up am exasperated and sink back. Prime location. Now all that matters about me is over and as I listen I think I believe this but there is a sound in the next room. Something moving. Not everybody but a slice.

Nov. 3. Sometimes the idea of going to the bathroom makes me sick. I feel ashamed for myself and everybody on this planet. If only something could be done about it. But it can't. So we have to go on doing it because we can't stop eating or drinking. We could stop thinking about it so much however and then maybe the shame of defecation and urination might gradually go away. You know, like a storm blows away. Sometimes we ignore the few amenities that are there, committed to boredom from behind. The salt taste of it pretty well dissolves into your sense of being. There isn't much to control any more. You know the blossoms, fed by facts, and they disappear in the night and there is a long wait for the fruit, and by then it has become a fact. You do not wait for facts. Nothing moves at night. So you are resisting, foretelling, and the casual amenities like a nice chair or dish are overlooked, dropping into the endless garbage chute of the present. Have a nice day.

Katonah Mar. 18. A reinvestigation and reappraisal of the whole situation was under way. They played "Moliendo Caffé" and several others of his favorite hits. It was that time of decade.

Mrs. Threnody was having Madam How and Lady Why in. They didn't understand. Mrs. T. was desperate. But, as panic results in calm, so accidents produce the blandness in which they may or may not decide to occur. Finally it is seen that they will have been in retreat a long time. On call, though absent.

Records succeeded one another tirelessly on the jukebox. Now it was a year or two earlier, the year of "C'est écrit dans le Ciel." And "Moustapha." What ever became of that guy? Bob Azzam? Whatever became of Sammy Kay, for that matter. And Shep Fields. But the man had wanted to speak. And all that he was able to get out was "thicity." He was talking about himself—his "authenticity"? Or "this city"? No, not likely. He'll probably be around again though.

8 mi to Danbury (Charles Ives). Can I believe it that I am back on this same freeway. What startles though is still the relation of the hills to the towns—their nearness. Their complete—yet benign—lack of cooperation. Bit of old Charlie there. Yet also—reminds me of certain people I know. You can't always trust those most in sympathy with you, with your ideals. Often it's the warmth and understanding you obtain only from the sliest of your enemies that is your life's blood, your symbol of why you are on earth.

Patchy conclusion to this: the fall flowers rotting. You must love your enemies. It's impossible not to. So don't expect any credit for it. You have already digested your reward.

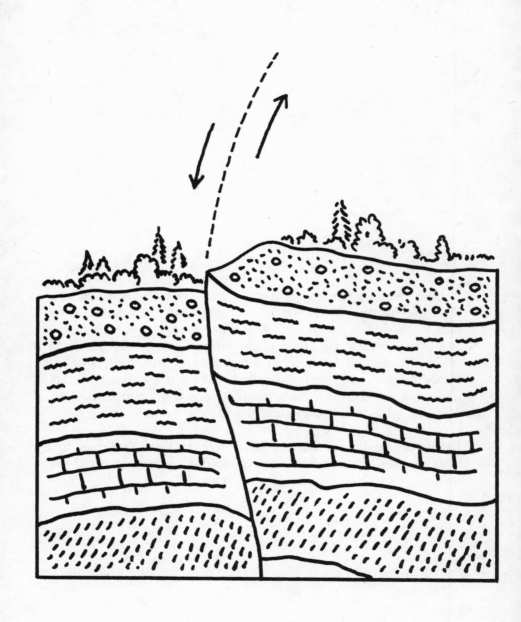

Somewhere we have taken off from, there seems no need to return, however desperate, motion sickness is enough. (Another list here.)

Call Southern New England Telephone Co.

Pitney Bowes—Alpex. Just what are these people (for I think they are people). Just how much am I expected to know about them? How interested should I get in them? Is there a place of turning off? But they say the calculator cannot find it. Yeh.

Things, copper sky, black trees. Some gracious some indifferent. The matter is: stones building up under the surface that finally swell and burst out into sunlight. Patient phenomena—well. Not really.

His sideburns. Problem about them. He liked them. They made him feel good. But nobody else did. They were too polite to say anything. But he knew they didn't like them. Still, he felt good, in an unusual sense of the word ''good,'' as in ''good night.''

The perils of just aimlessly sitting. Of having continually to go out and fix something. These never endanger us, but they condition us more than we know.

Little nuts, big nuts.

Asked for a conclusion, he paused long enough to be heard.

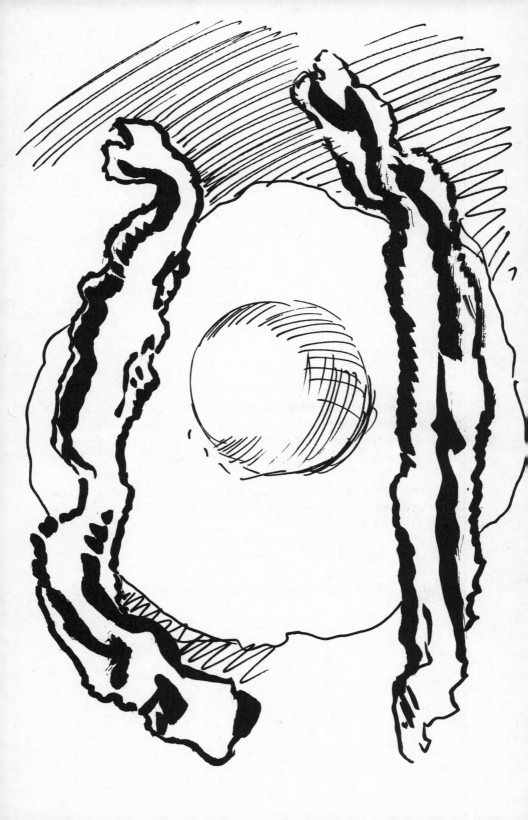

The water is sliding, now crawling delicately under the wax surface of the ice. In a little while it will be magnificently gilded. A ''sand trap.'' Her only food in five days: a dead chicken that floated by her on the water, which she ate raw.

They had a good idea when they named this place Plainville. Of course it *is* plain and it sits on a plain, but there are other facets of its plainness. It has a ''Poodle Parlor,'' from which schnauzers are not excluded, nor any dog not downright mad I should think. A table with magazines. Some of them dog-eared. Those who wish to wait for their pet's beautification may sit and read or not read, if they prefer. Or they may leave and come back in about an hour. Get the shopping over with. This is called ''theft of services.'' In the woods to the south of town are certain trees with bits of red cloth tied to them. Sometimes blue. Mostly red. The blue is found only rarely, if at all.

Man dreams of putting penis between girl's boobs. Is all mankind diminished? Or strengthened? What do you want? I want a pair of orange pants and a pair of orange and white shoes to go with them. I know nothing will work out unless I get them, but I also know that if I do get them I probably won't want to wear them to a dogfight.

Now—step back please. Man removes booger from nostril. Man examines booger. Man *relives* booger. All the shame. But could it have been avoided? Whatever has not been avoided probably could not have been avoided. One must learn to live with this possibly greatest of truths like sleeping over a garage.

Most of these buildings have been torn down now.

That shamrock button, t-shirt showing through the short-sleeved tattersall shirt, the way of looking around—not to be taken from behind, and to take, if possible, from ahead. So we call him their ''ringleader.''

Not to have passed this way in a very long time. And the next time? Places have a way of coming back; the full curve of expectation meets halfway one's pipsqueak pretensions starting out. Something happens out of this to protect it.

Think spring. We do. Slow down.

The waves were amazed.

America is a fun country. Still, there are aspects of it which I would prefer not to think about. I am sure, for instance, that the large "chain" stores with their big friendly ads and so-called "discount" prices actually charge higher prices so as to force smaller competitors out of business. This sort of thing has been going on for at least 200 years and is one of the cornerstones on which our mercantile American society is constructed, like it or not. What with all our pious expostulations and public declarations of concern for the poor and the elderly, this is a lot of bunk and our own president plays it right into the lap of big business and uses every opportunity he can to fuck the consumer and the little guy. We might as well face up to the fact that this is and always has been a part of our so-called American way of life.

Speaking of bunk....

Nevertheless, there are a lot of people here who are sincerely in love with life and think they are on to something, and they may well be right. Even the dogs seem to know about it—you can tell by the way they stick their noses out of the car windows sometimes to whiff the air as it goes by. Old ladies know about and like it too. In fact, the older an American citizen gets the more he or she seems to get a kick out of life. Look at all the retirement communities and people who mow their own lawns and play golf. They surely have more pep than their counterparts in Asia or Europe, and one mustn't be in too much of a hurry to make fun of such pursuits. They stand for something broader and darker than at first seems to be the case. The silver-painted flagpole in its concrete base surrounded by portulacas, the flag itself straining in the incredibly strong breeze, are signposts toward an infinity of wavering susceptible variables, if one but knew how to read them aright. The horny grocery boy may be the god Pan in disguise. Even a television antenna may be something else. Example: bearded young driver of pickup truck notes vinyl swimming pool cover is coming undone and stops to ask owner if he can be of assistance. Second example: groups of business people stranded in stalled elevator sing Cole Porter songs to keep their spirits up, helping each other recall the lyrics. Third example: a nursing home director convicted of a major swindle goes to the federal penetentiary for a period of not less than five years. Fourth example: you are looking down into a bottomless well or some kind of deep pool that is very dark with the reflected light so far in the distance it seems like a distant planet, and you see only your own face.

Some of these tunes hold up remarkably well. So, in the words of the song, I shall ''stay on the bus, forget about us, and put the blame on me.'' Unless you decide to ''tie a yellow ribbon round the old oak tree.'' (Corky sees me in the landfill and starts complaining.)

More seagull snapshots. You know they reduce to brownish blobs like old Bible camp photos. The beach is indeed one aspect of the vast Sunday school of the world, waiting for church to be over and go home. It has the look of openness to suggestion and the finished ultimate look that together characterize life. And the humor, is there anything mildly funnier than footprints on a beach. Life comes naturally there, and goes too: no sense worrying about naturalness with so much natural fuzz (fuss?) everywhere, in corners, in bushes, and the aired mystery of the open field (?). Briars come to ask you for ideas, and afterwards your blessing.

The forsythia is now out, marking the beginning of "little spring." In a certain way more of an attitude is possible in the face of winter—smell of boiled coffee and fried clams—because it knows it is on the pathway to nowhere. But to be again settling down like this in a torn silk parachute onto layers of dry half-rotted leaves, loam and anonymous rock outcropping, with here and there a portentous green shoot—does it make much sense to you. The "floods of spring" that are supposed to gurgle and gush impetuously are already sluggish and dark grey. The one comforting thing is all the leftover junk from last season, but this is fated to disappear shortly when Mother Nature starts her annual spring cleaning and "exterior" decoration. Meanwhile an uproar is supposed to be made over the first crocus popups and the like, daffodils that suggest public libraries, violets and the rest of the symbolic crap that is so much eyewash to divert our gaze from the ruthless pageant whose stage is now being hammered together out of raw lumber that will eventually be draped in yellow and green cambric, on which Josephine Preston Peabody's excruciatingly bad *The Piper* or something equally ominous of Percy Mackaye will shortly be enacted by the class of 1919.

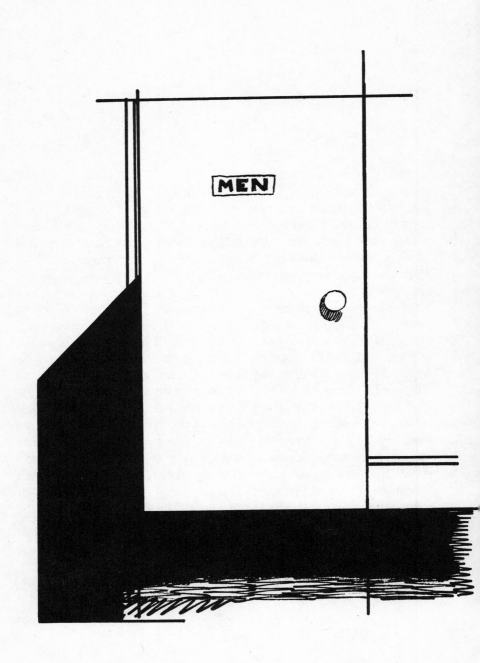

Did I know you, split-levels? What it's like to inhabit your dangerous divided spaces with view of celery plantations? The book sits there, alive with pleasure, but there is no more frontage. Fewer than a dozen of the sum of 32 flavors are kept in stock and you have to put a dime into a slot on the door of the men's room to get in. In other times "frontage" meant relief to enjoy, not a nameless dark forced familiarity with things. True, everybody was out then, on foot, on bicycle, or even in a horseless carriage, but this degradation of being forced out and around without thinking about it was only a shadow in the mind. Which gradually lengthened into late afternoon as the skyscrapers grew taller and taller, one by one, so that at present we have a density of blue twilight at high noon. Special vehicles are parked out of sight.

Once, speculators were briefly interested in these parallel bunches of needles. Now the bottom has dropped out from under them. They do move slightly in a metallic breeze that neither parches nor moistens. Many have been declared national park zones. A foreign student stands there, beyond the wire fence. His lips spell out the words: shale cowturds spread udder mumps.

To the Hard Barn Road Cafeteria

Bev would have loved it here. The rural look of everything, even city intersections. ('Mongst other things, they have the solid old-fashioned traffic lights—red, amber, green, where each color comes on and stays for its allotted due before blinking off, and no green directional arrows.) The landscape is countryish without looking countrified. In fact it looks as though it had its mind on more basic preoccupations, as though if it could talk it would say, "Sorry, I don't have time to think of such things." Up there of course is the subdued glow where McDonald's, Carrol's, Arthur Treacher, Colonel Sanders and Dunkin' Donuts succeed each other at the pace of a stately gavotte. But back here even this close all is already rubble and confusion—the country, in other words. Milk barns with the paint peeling off of them, long pale greenish-blue '66 Chryslers, a sense of gloom and desperation but also of seizing at final solutions. A riotous intoxicating feeling of freedom but so laced across with

conditions of terror that one enjoys it as something else, like the one night of freedom enjoyed by Louis XVI and his wife, after their escape from the Tuileries and before their capture at—wait, I know the name, I don't have to look it up—Verviers. Imagine the conditions of such a freedom, of not being able to enjoy a single second of it, enormous as it was, worrying about whether the milkmaid may have recognized you from seeing your profile on a coin. Here nobody is taking any chances on recognizing or being recognized. They all look like faces on Wacky Package stickers or a klutz in Mad Comics, tortured past reason and exploding in a human, all too human display of facial fireworks. This fools nobody but since it has become the unrecognized custom of looking, for these foolish folks who won't bother you and don't you bother them, it has a currency, a legitimacy, both thinner and more extensive than the lumpy look the rest of us have. The scenery looks as though it was painted on cork.

A recent fishing jaunt to the southern Gulf coast of Florida gave me the opportunity to visit with Dr. Jay L. Harmic, the scientist in charge of the long-range research program at Marco Applied Marine Ecology Station. Considerable progress has been made there in the initial three years of operation, and the prospects are excellent for environmental protection and improving the already fabulous fishing.

One of the projects causing a lot of excitement while I was there trying to concentrate on casting for spotted trout and reds, was the successful nesting of a pair of bald eagles in an artificial site. The Marco Ecology Station had moved a tree that had been abandoned by eagles to a new location where it was strapped to a concrete piling in a mangrove thicket. ''This gives us the encouragement we need to proceed further in location, saving and possible re-locating likely eagle nesting trees in the area,'' Harmic commented.

While finding ways to protect and enhance the environment for an endangered species like the bald eagle is making big news these days, it should be only a preview of what we might expect from the $750,000 ecology program being funded by the Miami-based Deltona Corporation, developers of Marco Island. The ongoing program includes general marine and mangrove island research, monitoring activities that keep a hand on the pulse of the environment, recommendations to Deltona concerning environmental protection, and replacement or enhancement projects.

Of primary importance to fishermen, is the program to develop a better off-shore fishery at Marco. The Marine Ecology Station, which has a staff of seven full-time marine scientists and technicians and a half-dozen part-time laboratory assistants, has created two artificial reefs to attract sport species. At a location one mile off Marco, 57,000 old automobile tires have been wired together forming an underwater structure. At another location four and one-half miles into the Gulf, some 5,000 tons of construction debris has been piled along the bottom.

Prior to the artificial reefs, studies revealed that one fish could be caught for every two hours of fishing effort. Right now fishermen are averaging between seven and eight fish per hour, and sometimes the count goes up to 15 fish per hour. Divers from the Station have recorded 87 different species of fish on the reefs, with the most numerous sport species being groupers and jacks.

Since biologists know the value of the mangrove islands to spawning fish such as snook and tarpon, the Station is now experimenting with the establishment of artificial islands. A large reference collection of marine life is being created, and some extremely valuable records on the dissolved oxygen in the water are being established. Another first at Marco, is that no sewerage effluent is returned directly to the water—after three stage treatment it is used to irrigate one of the golf courses.

Marco is an example of how a new community can be sensitive to the natural environment. One hopes there will always be nesting eagles, the mangrove wilderness, and jumping fish. And one hopes that other developments will take note.

This is where we are spending our vacation. A nice restful spot. Real camp life. Hope you are feeling fine.

Some days hell seems very near. As this on-again, off-again type day, fickle sunshine one moment and deep ugly black clouds the next. At these times you can hear a rustling from the next room, as though hell were about to break its own self-imposed rule of silence and speak, speak up in an urgent, quiet tone, reminding you of its existence and your own laziness, telling you to get on with whatever it is you're doing, even if it's just a crossword puzzle, for your own sake, because all times are getting close and so far there just isn't enough activity of any kind to justify the terribly solemn moment when all four draw near at the crossroads. Not that any justification is required. But it does make it better for them, to feel everything is proceeding according to plan. And it is. Therefore, whatever it is that you want to do, do it, and this way everybody's task will be made just a little bit easier. Though you may well be inclined to ask yourself, just the same, what exactly was it you did. It seemed to be nothing, and the minutes ticked by, cheerful, indifferent—and merely standing still you felt trapped in a sliding scale of a whole universe of judgments, positive and negative, and wondered where you stood to profit in the prearranged woodshed of doubtful possibilities, until a boy detached himself from the uninteresting landscape and came over and tapped on the window, restoring the sense of life's wholeness. That was an apology, but it worked. The lake is no longer restless and the railroad yards are straightened up. There are more cement igloos.

The Fairies' Song

Clouding up again. Certain days there is a feeling that whatever we
    arrange
Will sooner or later get all fucked up.
Then there are explosions of a 19th-century, garden-variety form of
    intellectual rage.
We have moved too far in the glade, the way this is all about
    harassing.

Sometimes one of us will get included in the trash
And end up petulant and bored at the multiple opportunities for
    mischief,
Screaming like a seagull at vacuity,
Hating it for being what it is.

There are long rides around doubtful walked-in spaces,
Dreaming manure piles under the slop and surge of a March sun,
Rivers of reeds, rivulets of webbed mud,
Pale plumes of dullness portentously fixed at the four corners of a
    moment of tearing around only to be caught out.

Thunderheads of after-dinner cigar smoke in some varnished salon
Offer ample cover for braiding two coat-tails together
Around the clumsy arm of an s-shaped settee.
In a screech the occasion has disappeared, the clamor resumed like a
    climate.

There are limpid pools of quiet
Offering themselves to the relaxed curve of a pebble,
Baskets of normal occurring, insipid flowering meads,
Wastes of acting out daytime courtesies at night,

Deadfalls of resolution, arks of self-preservation,
Arenas of unused indulgence. Where do we get off
The careening spear of rye? The milk meanwhile is soured
But it all gets mixed up in your stomach anyway.

We dance on hills above the wind
And leave our footsteps there behind.
We raise their tomatoes.
The clear water in the chipped basin reflects it all:
A spoiled life, alive, and streaming with light.

What lovely antiques . . . (fap, grunt). Isn't it funny the way something can get crowded clean out of your memory, it seems new to you when you see it again, although some part of your mind does remember, though not in any clear-cut way?

Dear Autumn Addict,

Have decided this bus trip will be good for my spirits. Am sitting next to a young man I saw in the terminal, who resembles a portrait by Carolus Duran, and whom I shall call "Oscar." "Oscar" is restless and plainly wants to smoke a cigarette, although there is a "No Smoking" sign. In some buses they allow cigarette smoking but no pipes or cigars, but this is an interstate bus and so maybe smoking at all is against the laws of one of the states the bus passes through. Anyway, "Oscar" as I call him for want of another name, keeps pulling a rather rumpled pack of Benson and Hedges out of his pocket, turns them over, stares at them or past me out of the window, stuffs them back in his pocket again. Hope that you are now settled permanently (?) in your new home you will pen your thoughts more often. As much as I do enjoy the many new writers, I feel a special bond with those I first started corresponding with when we moved here.

If I don't hear from you again, I shall wonder whether or not you got so wrapped up in your ''canning and freezing'' that you are either somewhere on a shelf full of preserves with a metal lid on your head or holing up with the frozen peas in your freezer compartment, from life to something else swiftly translated. Be of good cheer.

Beverly

Printed January 1975 in Santa Barbara and Ann Arbor
for the Black Sparrow Press by Noel Young and
Edwards Brothers Inc. Design by Barbara Martin. This
edition is published in paper wrappers; there are 250
hardcover copies numbered & signed by the author &
artist; & 26 lettered copies handbound in boards by
Earle Gray, signed by the author & artist, each
containing an original ink drawing by Joe Brainard.

John Ashbery was born in 1927 in Rochester, N.Y. He teaches in the graduate writing program at Brooklyn College. His books include *Some Trees* (1956), *The Tennis Court Oath* (1962), *Rivers and Mountains* (1966), *Fragment* (1969), *The Double Dream of Spring* (1970), *Three Poems* (1972), and *Self-Portrait in a Convex Mirror* (to appear in spring 1975). He has published one prose work, a novel written in collaboration with James Schuyler entitled *A Nest of Ninnies* (1969).

Joe Brainard was born in Salem, Arkansas. Grew up in Tulsa, Oklahoma. At age 32—now residing in New York City's Soho. Currently teaching at The School of Visual Arts. Next book: the collected *I Remember* (Full Court Press). Next exhibition: the fall of '75 (Fischbach Gallery).

Photo: David Kermani